LET NOTHING TROUBLE YOU

Eugene McCaffrey OCD

Let Nothing Trouble You

Teresa: the woman, the guide and the storyteller

St Teresa of Avila
Centenary Year
1515–2015

the columba press

First published in 2015 by
the columba press
55A Spruce Avenue, Stillorgan Industrial Park,
Blackrock, Co. Dublin

Cover design by Mary Plunkett
Cover image: Stained glass window Carmelite Church,
Clarendon Street, Dublin, Phyllis Burke
© Photograph: Edmund Ross Studios, Dublin
Origination by The Columba Press
Printed by Scandbook, Sweden

ISBN 978 1 78218 219 1

Second Printing

Contents

Chronology

1515   Teresa de Cepeda y Ahumada born in Avila, 28 March.

1528   Death of Teresa's mother, Doña Beatriz de Ahumada.

1535   Enters the Carmelite convent of the Incarnation in Avila.

1537   Makes her profession as a Carmelite nun.

1543   Death of Don Alonso, Teresa's father.

1554   Teresa's total conversion to the Lord.

1561–62   Starts to write *The Book of Her Life*.

1562   Foundation of St Joseph's, Avila.

1566–67   Writes *The Way of Perfection*.

1567–82   Foundation of sixteen other convents.

1567   First meeting of Teresa and John of the
          Cross.

1568   First foundation of the friars.

1573   Starts to write *The Book of Her Foundations*.

1577   Writes *The Interior Castle*.

1580   The reform is granted its independence.

1582   Teresa makes her last foundation, in Burgos.
Dies at Alba de Tormes on 4 October.

1622   Canonised by Gregory XV.

1970   Declared Doctor of the Church by Paul VI.

2015   Fifth centenary of her birth.

The Principal Writings of St Teresa

The Book of Her Life (her autobiography)

The Way of Perfection (written for her nuns)

The Interior Castle (the inner journey of the soul to God)

The Book of Her Foundations (history of the convents she founded)

Meditations on the Song of Songs (reflections on Scripture)

Poetry (31 surviving poems and verses)

Letters (468 surviving letters)

SPAIN

FRANCE

PORTUGAL

Bilbao

León

BURGOS
19 APRIL 1582

Zaragoza

PALENCIA
29 DEC 1580

SORIA
14 JUNE 1581

Barcelona

VALLADOLID
15 AUGUST 1568

Río Duero

Río Ebro

MEDINA DEL
CAMPO
15 AUGUST 1567

SEGOVIA
19 MARCH 1574

SALAMANCA
1 NOV 1570

Alcalá

PASTRANA
23 JUNE 1569

ALBA DE
TORMES
25 JAN 1571

AVILA
24 AUGUST 1562

Madrid

TOLEDO
14 MAY 1569

Río Tajo

VILLANUEVA
DE LA JARA
21 FEB 1580

Valencia

CARAVACA
1 JAN 1576

Río Guadiana

MALAGÓN
11 APRIL 1568

Córdoba

SEVILLE
29 MAY 1575

Río Guadalquivir

Ecija

GRANADA
20 JAN 1582

Muria

BEAS DE
SEGURA
24 FEB 1575

Palma

Almería

Málaga

THE FOUNDATIONS OF ST TERESA

The Foundations of St Teresa

St Joseph's, Avila 1562	Beas 1575
Medina del Campo 1567	Seville 1575
Malagon 1568	Caravaca 1576
Valladolid 1568	Villanueva de la Jara 1580
Toledo 1569	Palencia 1580
Pastrana 1569	Soria 1581
Salamanca 1570	Granada 1582
Alba de Tormes 1571	Burgos 1582
Segovia 1574	

Upon This Mountain

To call Teresa of Avila a saint tells us something about her, but to call her a Carmelite saint tells us much more. Teresa did not emerge from a religious vacuum, but from a rich spiritual tradition which existed three hundred years before she was born. She knew its story and was inspired by its history.

Carmelites take their name from Mount Carmel, a majestic promontory in the Holy Land jutting out into the Mediterranean, sacred to the memory of the prophet Elijah. It is a place of prayer, presence and communion. There, the first hermits came together, eight hundred years ago, seeking a simple lifestyle and dedicating their lives to prayer and meditation. Carmelites' roots are there, and from there the journey of every Carmelite begins.

Teresa was one of countless Carmelite saints and writers open to the Spirit, not afraid to explore new horizons and new ideas. 'Begin always anew' was her advice to the communities of her day. She had the rare gift of being able to preserve the beauty and richness of the tradition she had inherited and, at the same time, to transform it into something new and original. Today the Carmelite Order comprises two branches springing from the same stock, breathing with both lungs, bringing out of its storehouse new treasures as well as old. The spirit of the first Carmelites and the splendour of the sixteenth-century renewal enrich each other in a common bond of prayer, service and community.

The *Rule of St Albert*, common to all Carmelites, offers the gracious invitation to follow Jesus Christ and serve him with a pure heart. This is the call Teresa heard and followed: a love story. And, like every love story, it involves a journey into the land of heart's desire.

This book is a small tribute to St Teresa of Avila, five hundred years after her birth, celebrating her life, her achievements and the dream that inspired her.

The Call of the Beloved

Saints leave their footprints on the sands of time and their lives echo down through the years. Every saint is a lover, and lovers never grow old, their lives always fresh in every age. Such is Teresa of Avila, a woman of deep and affirming spirituality, who lived life to the full and encourages us to do the same. Her message is simple: the treasure we seek is closer to us than the air we breathe, deeper than our own heartbeat. The world within is more real and more beautiful than anything we see outside.

The desires of the heart call us beyond ourselves. But if we do not acknowledge the longing, we cannot begin the journey. The great thing is that we are not alone: the search is twofold. The Beloved calls, and in him our restless hearts can find the deeper meaning and peace for which they long. Teresa has been there. She can be our guide and lead us gently and lovingly into 'the deep heart's core', despite the fears and anxieties that so often hold us back.

She is the surest of guides and the most approachable. Nothing is more striking about Teresa than her humanity, written large on every page of her writings. We cannot separate the woman from the saint. She was a charming, attractive, witty woman. Her personality is larger than life, and it is the genius of that life that has endeared her to so many. The saints are not saints because they turned away from the world but because they embraced it, saw it as God's handiwork and were captivated by the love story of creation. God's temple is wherever God is, and God is everywhere.

> *Remember that the Lord*
> *walks among the pots and the pans.*

Teresa is undoubtedly an artless and spontaneous writer of spiritual and literary gems. But they also give her away: she *is* her writings, she wrote as she spoke, she spoke as she lived, and they are a faithful testimony to her dynamic spirit. We see a woman suffused with common sense, good judgment and a delightful sense of humour. A mystic with her feet on the ground, she knew how to make poetry, music and dance out of her spiritual experiences.

Teresa did not write to solve problems or to prove anything. Her concern was to bear witness to the reality of God's presence in her life and in the world, a presence that overwhelmed her and filled all things. God was involved in the very fabric of her existence, as real to her as the prelates and magistrates, the innkeepers and muleteers she encountered on her travels. She was a realist: a seeker of truth for whom the supreme reality was all that mattered.

Teresa fits as easily into the twenty-first century as she does into the sixteenth. Her struggles are ours. For a long time she resisted the call of the Beloved, wasting hours and energy in frivolous friendships and half-hearted efforts. She learned the hard way. Yet this warm, clear-eyed woman, who was as much at home in the kitchen as in the chapel, who prayed well and lived well, can offer us guidance, encouragement and a sense of reassurance.

This small book is not just about her message: it is about her spirit and the vision that possessed her. This is why, five hundred years after her birth, amidst the noisy confusion of our lives we can still be inspired by her words, disarmed by her laughter and guided by her wisdom. She wants us to know we are loved, that life has a meaning far beyond all our dreaming. Her words are proverbial and timeless: 'Let nothing trouble you, all things pass away: God alone suffices.'

Prayer to St Teresa

St Teresa of Jesus, Mother of Carmel,
you gave yourself totally to the way of love
and of unselfish service to others.
Teach me to follow you along the way of prayer,
so that, like you, I may be a servant of love.
Help me to be ever more aware of the great mystery
that lies deep within the interior castle of my soul.
Draw me into a new encounter with Jesus.
May he be my companion in prayer
so that I may open my heart to him
in a spirit of friendship and love.

You found God among the pots and the pans.
May I also know his presence
in the joys and struggles of my everyday tasks.
All things pass away except his unchanging love.
Help me to remember that he knows all things,
can do all things, and that he loves me.

A New Dawn

Teresa de Cepeda y Ahumada or Teresa of Jesus, as she liked to be called, was born on 28 March 1515 in the walled city of Avila, Spain, a city of stones and churches where even the olive trees have faith. 2015 marks the fifth centenary of her birth. Her life and achievements have earned her many titles – reformer, writer, foundress, saint of God and Doctor of the Church – and these, together with her warm human personality, her wit and single-minded courage, have made her one of the great women of all ages.

Teresa was not a born saint and she would be the first to admit it. Her strong, vibrant personality yielded only gradually to the workings of God's grace in her life. She was a woman of immense desires, indomitable courage and generous spirit. She loved life and all things human, and was not afraid of either her own weakness or her own strength. It is hardly any wonder that she has become one of the most endearing and most approachable of all Christian saints.

A Woman of her Times

Teresa lived in turbulent times, an age of exploration as well as of political, social and religious upheaval. Only twenty-three years before she was born Spain was united under Catholic rule, when, after eight hundred years of control, the Moors were expelled from Spain. The powerful and influential Jewish community was also under scrutiny, and the Spanish Inquisition came into being to search out and suppress any taint of heresy. Religion became a dangerous weapon in the hands of the new ruling class. At about the same time, Christopher Columbus discovered the Americas and a brand new world opened up, a world of immense wealth, greed and colonial expansion. Two years after Teresa was born, Martin Luther lit the flame of the Protestant Reformation, and within the space of a single generation the face of Europe had changed irrevocably.

Teresa was not immune to these events, nor did she wish to be. In many ways they defined her life and her spirit. Jewish blood ran in her veins, and her family did not escape the censorious eye of the Inquisition. Like Columbus, she too was an explorer but of a different kind: her world was the world of the spirit, the intimate abode of love and friendship where God and the human soul meet and converse. Although she understood Luther's passion for reform and knew only too well the reality of sin and human weakness, she was also well aware of the transforming power of grace and rested secure and confident in the reality of God's love and mercy. Teresa lived, as we do today, in the age of a great Church

Council. The years of the Council of Trent correspond with her own interior struggle to surrender herself wholeheartedly to God and to begin her great work of renewal within the Carmelite Order. Her own life of prayer and contemplation, and that of the small community under her care, is a luminous witness to the universal call for a new heart and a new spirit within the Church of her day.

> *God has so many enemies and so few friends,*
> *these few friends should be good ones.*

A Woman of Many Parts

Teresa lived many lives. She was born into a well-to-do and successful merchant family in Avila, the sixth child of Alonso Sánchez and his second wife, Beatriz de Ahumada. Her mother instilled a deep love of books in her daughter, something that influenced and defined Teresa's life. Teresa was a lively, intelligent child, richly endowed with natural charm and the ability to please. When she was thirteen her mother died; and her father, concerned about her lively nature, felt her education would be best served in the nearby Augustinian boarding school. She stayed there for eighteen months until her health deteriorated.

In 1535, at the age of twenty, in the chill of a November dawn, Teresa slipped away from home and entered the Carmelite convent of the Incarnation in Avila. When she entered, the place was full to overflowing, with a hundred and forty nuns living in a house built for half that number. Teresa was happy there and entered enthusiastically into the life of the convent. Two years later she made her religious profession; her new name was *Teresa of Jesus.* But once again her health broke down, this time so completely that she was on the point of death. Her recovery was slow and painful, and for the rest of her life she never knew a day of complete good health.

For the next twenty years Teresa lived 'on a stormy sea', dilly-dallying with God, torn by the countless distractions and the endless comings and goings within the convent. Yet, at the same time she felt an increasing call to prayer, to which she had always tried to be faithful, and to a more generous surrender to the life of the spirit awakening within her. In the end it was an encounter with a statue of the wounded Christ that broke the impasse and opened a flood of unexpected favours and contemplative graces. She fell headlong in love with God and there was no turning back. A new life and a new world opened up for her.

I must tell you how I long to do something for
God's service:
I cannot live much longer and I would not like
to spend the remaining years as idly
as I have spent those just past.

Foundress

Teresa was forty-three when the idea of the reform came to her. At first she did not take it seriously. Gradually, however, the dream became a reality. Despite bitter opposition from individuals and from both religious and secular authorities, the first enclosed Discalced Carmelite convent, St Joseph's, was founded in Avila on 24 August 1562. Even Teresa herself could not have realised the momentous step she had taken. A new dawn had been awakened.

The years spent in the convent of St Joseph were the happiest and most peaceful she had ever experienced. She imagined she would be there for the rest of her life. But a bigger providence was already at work. Five years later she was on her way to make her second foundation in Medina del Campo. It was here that she met for the first time her future collaborator and companion in the reform, John of the Cross. Other foundations followed in rapid succession, spreading across the length and breadth of Spain, from Burgos in the north to Seville in the south, a distance of some four hundred miles. Each foundation brought its own hardships: negotiations with civil and ecclesiastical authorities, local opposition, misunderstandings, financial worries, and exhausting journeys along dusty tracks in the stifling heat of summer or the bone-chilling cold of a Castilian winter.

Teresa and four ducats amount to nothing.
But Teresa, four ducats and God can do anything!

An Order of Friars

As part of her original plan, Teresa was given permission to set up two houses for friars, men who would carry the contemplative ideal wherever they went, at home or on far-off mission fields. This became a reality in 1568 with the foundation of the first house for friars in Duruelo, thanks in no small part to the charismatic leadership of John of the Cross, a man of exceptionally keen mind and deep sanctity; a year later a second house was founded, in Pastrana. Before she died in 1582, there were seventeen convents of nuns and fifteen of friars, stretching from one end of Spain to the other.

> *Where do you think a poor woman like myself,*
> *subject to others, without a farthing of her own*
> *or anyone to help her, found the means*
> *to perform such great works?*

Valiant Woman

For the last twenty years of her life, Teresa worked tirelessly to lay the foundations of the new venture to which she was called. Her last and most difficult foundation was in Burgos, a relentless saga that dragged on for months in the face of opposition, intrigue and failing health. Tired and ill, she knew the end was near and wanted to return to her beloved Avila. But it was not to be. A final act of obedience, one of the hardest in her whole life, brought her instead to Alba. Here, on 4 October 1582, she died, her body spent with toil, her spirit undimmed, repeating with simple and humble devotion, 'I die a daughter of the Church.' She was sixty-seven.

It was not the end. Her work had barely begun. The fire that burned in her great heart could not be contained within the turreted walls of Avila: her spirit and her message took flight, let loose upon the earth.

Teresa was canonised in March 1622, forty years after her death. In 1970 she was declared a Doctor of the Church, the first woman to be so honoured.

Her feast day is on 15 October.

What's in a Name?

One day, as Teresa was making her way along the corridor in the convent of the Incarnation, she saw a small boy standing at the foot of the stairs.

'Who are you?' the child asked her.

'I am Teresa of Jesus,' she said to him. 'And who are you?'

'I am Jesus of Teresa,' the child replied, and vanished.

On Eagle's Wings

It would be easy to get the wrong impression of Teresa as a writer from her own opinion of herself. When asked once to write another book, she pleaded: 'For the love of God, let me get on with my spinning and go to choir and do my religious duties like the other sisters. I am not meant for writing; I have neither the health nor the wits for it.' Nevertheless, she put aside her misgivings and acceded to the request. And the result was – *The Interior Castle*!

Teresa was all too conscious of her rough style, her lack of time and her poor memory. In fact, she never set out to write a book: practically all her writing was done at the request of others. She simply wanted to record her own experience or to instruct her sisters in the way of prayer. Once she had completed this task she felt she had fulfilled her obligation.

A Born Writer

The extraordinary fact is that a woman who was not a scholar, who wrote much as she spoke, mostly under pressure, produced such a large body of literary and spiritual classics. She seems to have belonged to that privileged few who can truly be called 'born writers'. Despite all the disadvantages of which she was all too aware, she has that rare gift of appealing directly to the ordinary reader as much as to scholars and literary figures. She was a reluctant writer to begin with, stealing the time from spinning, but once she set pen to paper she was on fire with inspiration. She never adopted a literary 'style'. Indeed, her particular genius stems from the fact that she wrote exactly as she spoke. Teresa was a conversationalist and all her books read like long letters. Her spontaneity gives a feeling of intimacy to her writing. While never dull or boring, she can at times – and she herself would be the first to admit this – be difficult to follow!

The first impression we get from her writings is of what a sensible woman she surely was, and how well she could say necessary things in simple, plain language. She had a quick and sensitive mind and a ready wit that make her an intensely human writer. Her creative imagination, coupled with that feeling for life and insight into people, is a quality of all great writers. She is totally honest, and she combines passion and enthusiasm with utter simplicity. This homespun texture of her style has delighted countless readers in every age since it first flowed so spontaneously from her pen.

Sometimes I grab pen and paper like an utter fool.
I have no idea whatsoever how I am going to begin
and what I am going to say.

Self-Portrait

With some writers it is possible to separate their teachings from their personality. Not so with Teresa: she *is* her writings. To read her is to know her. Practically every page bears the imprint of her forceful and vivid personality. She wrote out of her own experience, and the unique quality of her writings is that they reflect, in such a personal way, the richness of her spiritual journey. Her writings are her life, a faithful testimony to her dynamic spirit.

Teresa had no literary training as a writer. Basically, she knew how to write – and little else! She was indifferent to the rules of grammar and syntax. She wrote from popular speech in the Castilian dialect of the time, which she spelt phonetically, and her vocabulary was that of common usage. For the most part, her material flowed automatically from the general thrust of what she wanted to say; the ground plan became apparent only after the work was completed. Often enough she herself was unaware, except in a general way, of the overall structure of the book.

'I shall have to use a comparison'

All Teresa's writings teem with homely comparisons and vivid metaphors. They add colour and often a touch of humour to many of her ideas. Some, like the great allegories of the way, the castle or the garden, provide the basic structure for her more important books. Others, more casual and throwaway, are scattered across almost every page, adding wit and sparkle to many of her comments and observations: images of chess and bullfights, of caterpillars and butterflies, of diamonds and precious jewels, of plants, flowers and herbs.

> *How I wish I could write with both hands,*
> *so as not to forget one thing while I'm saying*
> *another!*

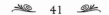

The Genius of her Life

But the greatness of Teresa is not in her style or in her wit, but in her sanctity. She was privileged to live and move in the presence of the living God revealed in the hidden depths of her own soul; to speak with him there and to share the intimate communion of divine life. Her writings are great – not for what they tell us of Teresa, but for what they tell us of God and of the reality of his love. Teresa not only experienced this divine friendship, but was able to record for us what she had seen and heard.

Since she struggled to make sense of her own spiritual journey, she is able to help us make sense of ours: the things that help and the things that hinder. She knows the road, she has been there. Her writings are full of light and encouragement; we are in safe hands. 'I want to see God' was her desire as a child, and it had set her on the road of life. That same desire lies deep in every human heart, and Teresa knows better than most how to nourish it.

Telling Her Story

Teresa liked to sing, dance and play the castanets. There was one refrain never far from her lips: 'To sing forever the mercies of the Lord.' It is a recurring theme in all her writings. In fact, she referred to her autobiography as the *Book of the Mercies of God*.

Her autobiography or *Life*, as it is called, is the story of her remarkable spiritual journey. Without it we cannot understand her life's work, her mission or her personality. The book is a work of candid self-revelation, written in a lively conversational style, which moulds itself quite naturally into a spiritual classic. This is all the more extraordinary in that it is her first attempt to capture her experiences in writing. The book makes an immediate impact, and even the most casual reader is captivated by her simple and picturesque language.

The Story of My Soul

There are many strands woven into the book: childhood memories, her first awakenings to God, her struggle to become a nun, and her discovery of prayer. She moves freely from the outward events of her life to the inner movement of the spirit. Personal details of her life overlap with historical facts relating to the beginning of her work as foundress; and at the heart of the book, a precious gem: her teaching on prayer, built around the metaphor of the 'four waters'. Many threads are interwoven within the story: portraits of her family and friends, youthful stories and anecdotes, tangled relationships, and friendships that were both dangerous and nourishing. We are given an endearing pen picture of Teresa herself, 'her father's favourite': outgoing, cheerful and charming, a natural leader, with an ability to please, a passion for reading books of chivalry and romance, wanting to be thought well of, and at the same time vain and fastidious about her appearance.

I began to dress in finery and to desire to please and look pretty, taking great care with my hands and hair and grasping at all the trinkets I could find to enhance my beauty.

The Garden of the Soul

However, the core of the early chapters is her discovery of prayer and her continual struggle to be faithful to it. Somehow, she admits, she had the courage to practise prayer but the slow, painful drama of self-conquest still continued. For twenty years, she endured the bitter struggle of trying to reconcile two contraries: her love for the world and her love for God; she wanted to surrender to God but did not know how. The struggle was all too real; she describes the repugnance she often felt at the thought of even going to the chapel and how she waited impatiently for the clock to strike!

But where the spirit of prayer grew stronger in her life, she breaks off her narrative and begins to write more explicitly about prayer. This is where she introduces her famous metaphor of the four ways of watering a garden. It is one of her most telling images, which she uses to explore the gift of prayer as it grows and develops in the human heart. It is a booklet within a book; it could stand on its own and is justly called a 'little jewel of prayer'.

Don't let anyone deceive you
by showing you a road other than prayer.

A New Life

Teresa opens the second section of her *Life* with the words: 'This is another new book from here on – I mean another new life ... the one God lived in me.' A new adventure begins: up to this point the life she has been living is her own; now she wants to write about the life God has begun to live in her. The graces and favours that came, unexpected and unforeseen, produced in her an overwhelming experience of the reality of God and his love for her which she could in no way doubt. Gradually she became aware of the constant and abiding presence of Christ in her life, engraved in the very depths of her being. The resulting explosion of love and her desire to do 'great things' for God could not be contained within the enclosed walls of a convent but exploded into action and a service of love: the foundation of the Carmelite reform.

The story of the foundation of St Joseph's, the first convent of the reform, is as remarkable as it is dramatic. At first, even she herself saw it as an impossible task; but our Lord had reassured her it would come to pass, urging her not to lose heart. And so it happened: despite public clamour and a storm of opposition from both civil and

religious authorities, the convent was founded. A new dawn had come to birth.

> *Not everyone is capable of meditating,*
> *but everyone is capable of loving.*

Her Own Woman

We must always be grateful that Teresa wrote her own life, told her own story. How easy it would have been for later biographers to polish the halo and undermine her humanity. She has eluded all efforts to tame or domesticate her, for her free and independent spirit radiates from every page. Some biographies record history, others create it. Teresa's *Life* stands on its own: she is not imitating others and she herself cannot be imitated. In the end, the life she lived is not about Teresa but about God who pursued and overwhelmed her. Her autobiography is an account of this encounter, his 'mercies' as she calls it; she simply relates what happened to her and how.

Although Teresa was fifty years of age when she finished her *Life* and had still many miles to travel and many battles to fight, she seems already to have had a profound insight into the meaning of her life, her future mission and the futility of all things that do not begin and end in the mystery and reality of God. She was lost and God had found her. A restless pilgrim, she had come home. 'God alone suffices.'

Who Do You Say That I Am?

'Do you know what they are saying about
me?'
Teresa asked one of her companions on the
way to Burgos.
'They say that in my youth I was beautiful,
then later they said I was clever
and now they are saying that I am holy.
There may have been a time I believed the
first two, but I have never been so deluded
as to even dream of believing the third;
such a thought has never entered my mind!'

A Catechism of Prayer

There's a story told about a man who spent most of his life looking for the perfect wife. When at last he found her, his offer was rejected: she was looking for the perfect husband!

The word 'perfection' does not rest easily on modern ears. Perhaps we are all too aware of our own human weakness and frailty as we struggle, each day, along the way of imperfection. Teresa may have felt the same about her book *The Way of Perfection*. It seems that it was only at the end of her life that she acknowledged the title, preferring mostly to refer to it as the 'little book' or the 'Lord's Prayer', for it contains her commentary on the 'Our Father'. 'Following the way of the Gospel' would seem to come closest in modern terms to what Teresa is really saying: inviting us to be friends of Christ and 'servants of love'.

A Way of Prayer

However, she was always happy to speak about the 'way of prayer' and, in the end, this is what the book is all about. She wrote it at the earnest request of the nuns who lived with her, and who had asked her to teach them about prayer and contemplation. It is a manual of practical advice and solid instruction in the following of Christ. She also wanted to explain the reason why she had founded a convent, and to share with them her vision for their way of life – adding casually that she will write about other things as they come to mind but has no idea beforehand what these might be!

The Way of Perfection is the most distinctly motherly and domestic of all her writings. More than any of her other books, it contains the dynamic spirit with which

Teresa herself was imbued. From start to finish it overflows with energy and enthusiasm, and with a burning desire to do great things for God.

> *Try to be as pleasant as you can,*
> *and get on well with those you have to deal with.*

Conversation with Christ

For a book written in such a seemingly casual manner, it is surprisingly well arranged and ordered. The theme of prayer gives it its basic unity. From the beginning she sees prayer in terms of friendship with Christ and service of the Church. God has so many enemies and so few friends, therefore, for Teresa, it is essential that these few friends be good ones. It is not the secular arm that will stem the tide of revolt or renew the Church, but earnest prayer and faithful love.

One of Teresa's favourite themes is the relationship between prayer and life, which is why she speaks so strongly about the basic human virtues: love for each other, detachment and humility. The value of prayer is in doing it, not in thinking about it. We can open ourselves to God in many ways, as long as we do so attentively. We can pray with words or without them, in silence or in meditation, or simply rest in his presence.

> *Do not talk to God and think about*
> *something else.*

The 'Our Father'
Teresa's teaching on the 'Our Father' is one of the best known of all her writings, and deservedly so; perhaps, as has been suggested, the most beautiful commentary on

the 'Our Father' that has ever been written. The 'Our Father', Teresa shows us, is a little catechism of prayer in which the Lord teaches us the whole way of prayer and contemplation. For Teresa, each petition of the 'Our Father' opens up new horizons of friendship and intimacy with God as she masterfully weaves her ideas around the words of Jesus, who taught us this prayer.

The ideas and images Teresa uses in *The Way of Perfection* are part of everyday life and have a global appeal. Prayer is not just a few quiet moments before a lighted candle, but a heart-filled attitude that permeates our entire life. Prayer is a refusal to shrink from life's challenges. By its very nature it creates community, friendship and love; after all, humanity is the measure of our relationship with other people. It is an open road along which every Christian is invited to walk, an invitation that echoes the universal call to holiness proclaimed by Vatican II. Every Christian is called to persevere as a faithful soldier of Christ, to face the challenge of life 'head on', fired with great desires and strong determination.

> *It would be a bad business if we could pray*
> *only by going off by ourselves into a corner.*

A Gospel Call

The Way of Perfection is universally acknowledged as a book for all seasons, its scope extending far beyond the small community of the ten or twelve sisters for whom it was originally intended. It is a catechism of prayer and a manual of Christian living. Prayer, in whatever form it takes, is a call to growth, friendship and love. Teresa's witness is clear and inspirational; she speaks from experience in a way that is fresh and encouraging. Her words have a liberating effect: they expand the heart, open doors that we didn't even know existed, and reveal a world of transforming beauty and joy.

Teresa concludes by saying that she will be well rewarded for the labour of writing if anyone finds the book helpful. Four and a half centuries later, the reward is ours: we are the ones who have received a treasure.

A Dwelling Place Within

Life is a journey, and in the end it is the journey itself that matters. The greatest journey of all is the journey within. It is not one of many steps but of deep longing. Not knowing how close the treasure is, we seek it far away. Yet it is only a heartbeat away; the world within is more real and more beautiful than anything we can see without.

Teresa's *Interior Castle* is a priceless guide in this great adventure of the soul's inner pilgrimage to God. It is the last of her major works, written five years before she died. It was started, appropriately, on Trinity Sunday and completed six months later. It was written against the background of what was undoubtedly the most difficult period of her life: she herself was forbidden to leave her convent and her life's work was in danger of collapse. Yet, incredibly, despite all the hostility and bitter opposition, she wrote what is now regarded as a literary and spiritual masterpiece.

The truth is that the treasure we seek
lies within our very selves.

At the Door of the Castle

Teresa admits that she had no idea what she was going to write about until God showed her a most beautiful crystal globe, made in the shape of a castle, and containing seven dwelling places. In the seventh and innermost dwells the King of Glory, in the greatest splendour, beautifying them all. The meaning was clear and the essential structure of the book fell into place: the castle is the soul, with God at its deepest centre, and the journey inwards is an invitation to explore the various rooms and dwelling places of the 'interior castle'.

From the outset the focus is on growth, beauty and endless possibilities. For Teresa it is the journey that matters most; the castle is not a fixed, static entity but something living, spacious and open. The rooms of the castle are not ready-made: we are given the tools, we are given possibilities, we are given dreams. We must be adventurous: the dream can only be realised once we have the courage to begin. It is the first step that matters; the path opens up as we travel. Each dwelling place in a sense contains all the others and, like a hologram, reflects and mirrors the changing pattern of the inner journey.

Love cannot possibly be content
with remaining always the same.

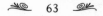

Light and Darkness

Teresa is also very conscious of the darker reality, the negative side of the Christian experience. To be transformed by the light of Christ involves a struggle with contrary and opposing forces: the enemy within. She acknowledges the difficulties, obstacles and hindrances, coming from what she calls 'snakes and vipers and poisonous creatures'. With such graphic images she acknowledges the inner forces pulling against the soul. The battle is all too real; the emerging light struggles with the inner darkness.

Teresa has great sympathy for those setting out on the inner journey. She is all too aware of the struggle between the first stirrings of an awakened love and the welter of attractions arising from a self-indulgent past. This is a time for planting seeds – seeds that in their own time and place will flower and bear fruit. There is a beginning of a relationship with God, however tenuous, and an awareness of a deeper hunger and thirst which, up until now, has hardly been noticed. God is working quietly in hidden and unexpected ways; a deeper providence and design is taking place.

> *The Lord does not look so much*
> *at the greatness of our deeds*
> *as at the love with which we do them.*

Call to Surrender

These early dwelling places represent a kind of conversion, a facing inwards rather than outwards. Deeper longings echo within and the spirit grows stronger and more resolute. Most people start well, living careful, well-ordered lives but then become complacent and fall into routine. The good becomes the enemy of the better. Difficulties in prayer and the challenge of the gospel demand discipline and more personal commitment. It is not easy to be patient, Teresa observes, when the door of our heart is closed and we are not able to enter into the presence of the Lord. Only those who really listen and surrender will hear the deeper call and respond.

For Teresa everything revolves around the fourth dwelling place. It is a place of transition; here, a terrible beauty is born and the whole spiritual landscape changes. A chasm has opened up, one that we cannot cross by ourselves. We are no longer in control: we have to be led, carried like a child in its mother's arms; the inner spring has found a new source. She is speaking about the beginning of contemplative prayer: a way of seeing, and of 'being', in relation to God – a free and boundless gift. God has begun to act more directly in the human heart, transforming it into his own image and likeness. New and deeper vibrations of the spirit are at work and we are being asked to enter by the narrow gate.

> *We have heaven within ourselves,*
> *since the Lord of Heaven is there.*

A Little White Butterfly

Essentially, this experience is an invitation to intimacy and personal friendship with God. Nothing is more real than God's love poured into the heart by the Holy Spirit. It is like the experience of 'falling in love' – being caught up in an embrace of divine friendship. Horizons expand, friendship deepens, and the soul is being transformed into an unshakable love: love of God and love of neighbour.

Teresa is renowned for her use of graphic images. One of the most famous of all her images, certainly one of the loveliest, is that of the silkworm and the butterfly. The soul reborn in Christ resembles the caterpillar transformed into something that could never have been imagined: a white butterfly – free, beautiful, yet fragile. Teresa needed this image. The image of the castle was not creative enough for her. It did not allow the sense of freedom and growth that she wanted to speak about. The soul has been liberated, has shaken off the bonds and is no longer earth-bound.

The best place to find God is within yourself.

Finding God at the Centre

For Teresa the innermost and deepest centre of the soul, the 'second heaven', is God's own dwelling place, an abode of peace. But it is not a surface peace, a state of bliss or of unruffled calm. Love explodes in a surge of spiritual energy and unselfish service. For Teresa, her duty as foundress was far from finished; there was still bitter opposition to her work, her health was in decline, she had many more roads to travel, other convents to found, and endless administrative burdens. She was a pilgrim in the service of the Beloved, she was a fool for Christ. It is little wonder she speaks of Martha and Mary. They need each other, together they express the fullness of Christian life: love in service, flowing from the hands of Martha and the heart of Mary. Love cannot show itself apart from deeds of love.

But at the heart of the castle, Teresa discovered something she could never have imagined, not even in her wildest dreams. What was revealed was not just the presence of Christ but an encounter with the living God revealed in the very heart of the mystery of the Trinity. The culmination of the great journey inwards was for Teresa an entry into the triune nature of God: oneness hidden in the heart of the Trinity. What she once accepted by faith she now understood by inner sight.

Journey's End

Teresa has shared with us not only a journey but a dream: God's dream for us. There is a call, an invitation; the only limitation is the horizon of our own vision. God's dream for us is greater than anything we can imagine for ourselves. We are the castle, it is real and it is within. We are called to grow, to explore the wonders hidden in our own heart. The Beloved is waiting to be our guide and companion. All we have to do is *want* to want him, to take the first step, and to follow the well-marked path through the darkness and into the light.

Who Needs Enemies?

Teresa was on the way to make her last foundation in Burgos. She had been advised not to go as it had been raining solidly for days and the roads were almost impassable, but she was convinced that the Lord wanted the foundation and that he would look after them. As they neared their destination the road became more treacherous and they were in danger of being swept away by the force of the water. As the floods rose higher and higher they had to battle to keep their footing and they were convinced that they were about to drown. In the end, they just managed to struggle to safety and journeyed on exhaustedly to a dry piece of ground.

Teresa immediately rounded on God: 'Lord, we almost drowned! Why did you let it happen? We are only doing what you asked us to do?'
The Lord answered her: 'Teresa, this is how I treat my friends.'
To which she retorted: 'Well then, it's no wonder you have so few!'

A Restless Gadabout

'A restless gadabout' – this was how the Papal Nuncio described Teresa! And he was right: she *was* restless – restless for God! If only he could have read her *Book of the Foundations*, he might have come to understand the fierce, wild passion that drove her along the winding roads of Spain, following the divine call and fired with a burning love for the Lord.

If you examine the matter carefully,
you will see that these houses
were not founded by human effort
but by the mighty hand of God.

A Great Adventure

Teresa made seventeen foundations during her life, all of them for women. To these we can add several houses for men which were founded under her influence. The book detailing these foundations had no title, partly because Teresa herself was unsure of what sort of book she was writing: a diary, a historical record or a long, newsy letter to her sisters! For someone who claimed to have a poor memory and a bad head for dates, she is remarkably accurate and reveals herself to be a marvellous storyteller. Nothing is insignificant, she has a keen eye for detail, and is a shrewd observer of human nature. She records the important as well as the trivial, and delights in sharing the things that made her smile and that she knows will entertain her readers. Here, as in her letters, we see the real Teresa, mixing jest and story, drawing colourful portraits of the great and the humble, now forever immortalised in her words and stories.

> *Thank God, there will be no changes of weather in heaven!*

A Book of Praise

From the start it is obvious that her accounts were made to be listened to rather than read: Teresa speaks with simplicity, as she would among friends, and seems to relish the idea of telling the story of each foundation. Her personality shines through every line. We see a woman filled with God, a captivating human being who comes to life as she chats away charmingly about her travels. Yet although the book gives a marvellous snapshot of Teresa herself and records her ingenuity and tireless efforts in making these foundations, this is not essentially what she had in mind. What she really wanted was to glance backward in a hymn of gratitude and praise to 'His Majesty', for it was all his work. In fact, she ends her book with a prayer of thanksgiving: 'Blessed be God who devotes so much care to all that concerns his servants.'

So sure is she that God is the inspiration and source of everything, that the work reads more like a book of blessings than an account of recollections or journeys; it is as much a book of prayer as a book of history. She is more concerned to describe how the Lord advised, planned and brought everything to fulfilment, rather than to specify historical events. For Teresa, it is all part of the record of his mercy and providence. He is the architect, the designer and the instigator of every foundation, 'the master of the rents and tenants'. It is he who makes friends, and sometimes strangers, comes to her rescue in a time of direst need. She listens to the Lord, whether buying a house, dealing with magistrates or settling a case of law. He is her travelling companion on every journey that winds its way along the rugged, interminable roads from Avila to Seville.

> *Lord, if this is how you treat your friends*
> *it is no wonder you have so few!*

Telling the Story

God made the world because he likes to listen to our stories! He must have been delighted with Teresa's storytelling, stories told with beguiling charm, humour and utter simplicity. It is like a 'pilgrim's guide' to those searching for a God who really cares, and who turn to him with absolute trust and confidence.

In her chatty, informal style, the book is full of stories, anecdotes and events, small and great, vividly captured in simple, intimate language. Some of these are humorous, some poignant, and some almost incredible. There are also many asides: words of wisdom and of encouragement for her readers. As with the Gospels, the good news is contained within the telling of the story.

May the Lord deliver us from sour-faced saints!

A Spiritual Odyssey

Teresa's account of the foundations is one of the most endearing of all her writings. It is impossible to classify – a chronicle, a diary, a memoir, a family history, or an interesting travel book! It stands as a personal testament to her burning love for Christ and her passion for the spread of his kingdom. Her journeys were pilgrimages of faith. Each new convent was intended as a powerhouse of prayer where his friends, though few, would be good ones. Her convents, though small, would be communities of love and intercession for an embattled Church and a broken, fragile world.

Self-Portrait

Naturally, we get a lot of personal details about Teresa herself. She is unashamedly honest about her fears and concerns, her joys and disappointments. The book is set against the wider social and religious climate of the time, as convents are established in the harsh reality of squabbles, jealousies and the endless scheming of those who opposed her. Teresa had to find her way around a minefield of self-important officials, pompous prelates and unscrupulous landlords. But she knew what she wanted and, more often than not, she got it. She became an astute businesswoman, skilled in negotiations, lawsuits and legal contracts.

Yet it is the humanity of Teresa herself that transforms every event and every line of the book: a feisty, gritty woman, full of courage, humour and common sense. Against impossible odds she achieved something beautiful for God and built a monument more lasting than bronze. Up and down the dusty roads of Spain she travels, a woman with a mission, a servant of love: the one who tells the story and the one who makes it happen.

Your Servant, Teresa

'I just live for letters,' Teresa wrote to one of her nuns, and yet to someone else she complained about 'this continual letter-writing, the worry of which is killing me!' I suppose we've all been there, even if today it's emails and text messages that drain our energy.

Woman of Letters

Teresa wrote countless letters, perhaps thousands! Most of them belong to the years associated with her work as foundress as she kept in touch – often daily – with her Carmelite sisters and friends. These provide a rich insight into her own life as well as being a significant historical record of the period. They show us how she thought and felt, how she spoke and how she related to others. The diversity and range of the people with whom she corresponded is quite extraordinary: from her king to the general of the Order, to bishops, nuns, friars, friends and family.

In a sense, to know Teresa we have to read her letters. They reveal her personality more accurately than any of her other writings and give a fascinating picture of the intricacies of the reform and of the religious and social life of her time. The same is true of the variety of topics she covers: she shares family news with her relatives, offers support and encouragement to her nuns, complains about her health, and is not above administering a reprimand or showing her anger and frustration at the scheming and intrigues of her enemies.

It is a test of love
if we can put up with the shortcomings of others
and not be shocked.

A Skilful Administrator

Most of her letters were written far into the night by the light of an oil lamp, frequently after a long day of business or travel. Often she wrote in haste, never bothering to read over them. When necessary because of illness or tiredness, she used a secretary. Teresa used the ever-available muleteers to send her letters, but sometimes friends would deliver them for her. In her letters we see the extraordinary grasp she had of every detail of the reform but we also realise the enormous toll her conflicts with those in authority had on her health.

Teresa kept in constant touch with her convents through her letters but she also wrote to relatives, friends and a whole gallery of helpers and supporters on a regular basis. Her letters generally deal with business affairs and everyday events: some of great importance, such as the establishing of houses, concerns about finances, hiring workmen, appeasing landlords; others, more prosaic – even down to ordering food and gathering herbal remedies and cures for her sisters!

> *I beg you to ask God to make me a real nun – better late than never!*

A Woman of Charm
Letters were Teresa's natural medium. Every letter is a conversation, often animated, always personal and direct, never dull. They reveal facets of her personality which we

would otherwise never have known about. As her letters were personal and private, she was free to write without the censorship that so often overshadowed her books. Here we see her in a unique light: practical, patient, worried, teasing, sparkling with laughter and wit. Whether she writes to the bishop, to her confessor, to her Carmelite sisters or to any one of her countless acquaintances, she writes with a deeply human touch and with an obvious love and affection for others.

The great gift of Teresa's letters is not what they tell us about her activities, her journeys or the vast galaxy of people she met, but that, more than any of her other writings, they offer an unsurpassed portrait of Teresa herself. In speaking to others, she inevitably throws the strongest light on herself. Every letter bears the indelible imprint of just how profoundly human she was, and offers a window on her lively, intelligent, caring personality.

*Remember that you are not made of iron
and many good brains have been ruined through
overwork.*

A Saint with a Backbone

The vitality and honesty of her letters is a refreshing antidote to the stereotyped image we so often have of saints. We see her without a halo, a woman not afraid to be herself: fussing over her friends, annoyed at not hearing from them, delighting in the smallest of gifts, not above enjoying gossip, and acknowledging her need for friendship. We also see a business woman of genius, a skilled administrator, who consulted widely and took great pains with legal documents. She is never afraid to speak her mind even to the king, daring to remind him that 'even though Saul was anointed, yet he was rejected', and subtly suggesting to the general of the Order that 'even though women are not good at giving counsel, we sometimes hit the mark!' Every inch a spirited woman, a saint with a backbone!

> *Believe me, I understand the contradictory ways of women better than you do!*

But perhaps the chief value of her letters is the fact that we see someone who could balance, with such freedom and lightness of touch, an intimate friendship with God and an exhausting involvement with everyday affairs. Her letters are a challenge to every false separation between God and the things of God; nature and grace are brother and sister, gathering every human quality into the service of God.

A Good Night's Sleep

When my companion found herself shut up in the
room, she did nothing but look around her
fearfully. The devil must have helped her by
putting thoughts of danger into her mind in order
to upset me, for with my weak heart, very little is
needed to do this.

'What are you looking for?' I asked. 'Nobody can
possibly get in here.'

'I'm wondering,' she said, 'what you would do all
alone if I were to die now!'

If this happened it would certainly be a dreadful
thing; and it made me reflect for a moment, and
even frightened me a little.

'Well, sister,' I replied, 'I will consider what to do
when the occasion arises: now, let me sleep!'

As we had already had two bad nights, sleep soon
took away our fears.

Prayer of the Heart

Prayer has always been part of the Carmelite story: embedded in its DNA, rooted in its history. No one knew this better than Teresa and, although she felt she was not always successful at her prayer life, she always tried to be faithful to it. In the end, prayer was the touchstone and springboard for all her undertakings. It was not so much that she discovered 'a way of prayer' as that she realised that prayer itself is the way. The road to peace is peace; the road to prayer is prayer. Prayer is God's gift to those who pray. Prayer itself teaches us how to pray. It is not just one more thing with an outlandish name: it is what we are and who we are.

Awareness

'I can't pray, can't meditate, my mind is always wandering …' Does it all sound familiar? Certainly it was for Teresa, as she tells us of her own efforts to pray. Trying to control her wandering mind, she said, was like living with a madman in the house! In fact, she admits that until she came across what she calls 'the prayer of recollection' she never knew what it was like to find satisfaction in prayer.

'Awareness', 'mindfulness', 'attentiveness' are all words we are familiar with today. Teresa loved these words, too. She spoke about keeping our minds attentive and aware during prayer. Attitude is more important than thoughts, more important than the words we use. How simple her advice: 'Don't talk to God and think about something else!' When we speak to God it is only right to be aware of whom we are addressing and what we are saying. The whole thrust of her teaching on prayer is towards simplicity and a personal friendship, establishing an open and a receptive heart, focused and attentive to his presence.

> *We do not have to raise our voice*
> *in order to be heard.*
> *He is always at our side.*

Companionship

Prayer, for Teresa, is really a question of companionship. In fact, she found the best remedy for the fickle wandering of the mind was to focus on the presence of Christ. He is not just at our side – he is there living within our heart, teaching us to pray and, even more importantly, praying with us to the Father: 'He is never so far away that we have to raise our voice to be heard.' And if it helps, Teresa also says, don't be afraid to use an image or a book or a gospel scene. We all have our own favourites; she herself loved to sit with the woman of Samaria, talking to Jesus at the well and asking for the living water which he offers. Prayer, at its most essential, is friendship with Christ: keeping him company, talking to him often, in a heart-to-heart conversation of love.

Presence

The idea of presence is central to prayer: awareness that God is within, up close and personal. It is not a question of words but of silence, attentiveness and listening. Teresa speaks about a sea voyage: if there is a favourable wind we can journey more quickly and more directly than by land. She makes the same point with her favourite image of water drawn from a well, rising spring-like from within and overflowing into the heart. The important thing is not to think much, but to love much. It is all a matter of simplicity and of focusing. There is nothing small or self-centred about it; this is prayer that opens the heart in generosity of service, awakening compassion and love for others.

> *The Lord helps us, he strengthens us,*
> *and he is a true friend.*

Silence and Stillness

Teresa would have made a natural headmistress! She certainly was too good a teacher not to spell out practical advice – not in a formal, textbook way, but from her own experience. She only wanted to give encouragement and support, but her suggestions are as helpful as they are personal: an ABC for beginners.

First of all, she invites us to 'be aware': aware that 'the Lord is within and we should be there with him'. The

image of the 'interior castle' captures what she has in mind: a dwelling place of priceless beauty, a whole world of wonder waiting to be explored. What lies within is far greater than what lies without. We must not imagine the castle of the soul as dark or empty: it is a universe on its own, a vast world of light and beauty. We need no wings to go in search of it: all we have to do is to look within, with eyes of love, and open our hearts to the call of the Beloved.

But perhaps the greater challenge is to 'be still': to hold the mind hushed in silence, steady as a flame in a wordless place. Teresa knew only too well from her own experience the constant struggle of trying to settle the restless heart and the butterfly mind. In our own world of noise, stress and over-stimulation, there is even greater urgency today to find quiet spaces and oases of silence, not just for prayer but simply for survival! This urgent search for silence finds expression in the popularity of meditation classes, mindfulness courses and centring prayer. Acknowledging our own need for stillness and a quiet space will go a long way to opening the heart to the sort of prayer Teresa has in mind.

> We need no wings to go and search for him,
> we have only to look at him
> present within us.

Conversation with Christ

Teresa, we know, was a great talker. We can hardly imagine her ever stuck for words in any situation! In fact, she admitted it was one of her biggest problems. But it may also have been one of her greatest gifts. For her, prayer and friendship went together: intimate, easeful sharing with the One who she knew loved her. But it doesn't always have to be in words: 'He is never so far away that we have to raise our voice to be heard.'

As always, her advice is simple: talk to him, as best you can; if you can't, just stay there, let yourself be seen, and don't try too hard to do anything else! There is no need for long meditation or reflection: you have only to look at him with the eyes of the soul. Teresa speaks tenderly of the 'lovely, compassionate eyes of Christ' gently turned towards us awaiting our response of love. Rest in his presence. Do not imagine him far away, so far that we have to go to heaven in order to find him.

We have heaven within ourselves,
since the Lord of Heaven is there.

Open Road

For Teresa, prayer is not an optional extra. Neither is it a task or a burden – nothing kills prayer so much as a sense of duty. It is always an affair of the heart; like poetry or music, it touches the heart before it touches the mind. It is not a question of squeezing prayer into our day; it's a matter of building our life into our prayer. It should be as personal as our fingerprints or our voice. We don't need a reason to pray, but we do need a heart filled with longing and love. For Teresa, prayer is an open road, the 'king's highway' along which everyone can travel. There are no conditions, no limits, except those we impose on ourselves. All we need is the desire to pray, a quiet place and a sense of adventure!

Ask and You Shall Receive

One day when I was in prayer, begging God
to give us a house ...
He said to me: 'I heard you; leave me alone.'
I was as happy about this as if I already had
the house, and very soon I did!

Only a Woman!

Today is a time of painful transition for women within the Church. The promise of greater freedom, equality and genuine mutuality has not yet been realised, and many women still feel excluded from leadership roles and from decision-making within the Church. The situation today may be vastly different from that of the sixteenth century in which Teresa lived, a century which was hardly the most liberating as far as women are concerned, but the sense of exclusion still remains and the struggle to be heard is all too real.

How did Teresa feel about her own situation, and how did she cope with the limitations and constraints placed on her by the social and ecclesiastical structures of her day? Can such a loyal, docile daughter of the Church have

anything in common with those who today are crying out
to have their voices heard and their gifts recognised?

> Since the world's judges are sons of Adam and
> all of them men, there is no virtue in women
> they do not hold suspect!

Strong and Determined

Teresa was a strong and sophisticated woman in an age
when it was not acceptable for women to be strong and
sophisticated. Their role was seen as one of submission
and compliance. Yet she refused to be inhibited by the
conventional behaviour expected of women, and her life
is a striking example of how she used her talents and
abilities for the service of others. She knew how to live
within the confines of the establishment; she could deal
lightly with an unwarranted rebuke: 'None of this

bothered me that much, but I acted as if it did. I did not want to give them the impression that I was not taking what they were telling me to heart!' Teresa lived from the centre, which gave her a sense of confidence and assurance to speak boldly about what she most passionately believed in. She longed to be able to speak openly about the greatness of God and of his mercy, and made no secret of the fact that she was envious of the freedom men have to spread the good news and speak of the wonders of his love.

Called to Freedom

In some ways, it could be easy to get the wrong impression of how Teresa sees herself as a woman: 'Just being a woman is enough to make my wings droop, let alone the fact that I am such a wicked one!' Yet this 'wicked woman' was privileged, as few have been, to walk and talk with God, to enter into his presence and be transformed by her intimate relationship with him. Within this friendship she found an inner freedom and a sense of self-worth that can only come from deep interiority. Teresa was gifted with extraordinary wisdom, a wisdom that did not come from books but from reflection born out of the womb of personal experience. Despite the restriction of sanctions and hostile criticism she asserted the dignity and potential of women, inviting them to find their own spiritual path and to trust their own experiences. For Teresa, women as much as men are called to full human and spiritual maturity without being automatically stereotyped because of role or gender.

Oh, if you could see how full of scruples I am today!
I am very wicked and the worst of it is,
I never get any better.

The Human Face

Too often we see Teresa as the great mystic and reformer and miss the human face with all its changing beauty and that special quality of love and simplicity that marked her as a woman. Her letters, especially, stand as a record of the tenderness and compassion that flowed from a woman's heart. She never ceased to love family and friends and needed their friendship as much as she needed time for prayer. She was sometimes desperately lonely, complained about not hearing from people, and was frustrated at what to her seemed indifference or neglect by others. The Lord, she said, walked among the pots and the pans. So did Teresa herself; like most women at the time, she was quite at home in the kitchen. She was an excellent cook, fussy about cleanliness, and often during her travels collected new recipes for the sisters.

When they say someone is a saint,
you can be sure they are talking nonsense!

A Woman's Way

She is always quick to defend women: 'Jesus found more faith and no less love in women than in men.' She reminds one of the friars that women are not that easy to get to know; nor should he be too surprised at this since, she admits, women do not always understand themselves! One of the reasons she agreed to write her final book, *The Interior Castle*, is because she was writing for her own Carmelite sisters, and women best understand the language spoken between women.

Teresa's writings abound with images and metaphors, many of them distinctly feminine. Words could not adequately convey the full meaning of what she wanted to express. Beginning with the image of the castle, which is also in itself a symbol of the womb, she traces the soul's journey towards wholeness and the birth of something new and beautiful. The same idea is vividly captured in the symbol of the silkworm and the butterfly: life and death transformed into love. Marriage, of course, is her most profound symbol, expressing surrender and transformation: a place where lovers meet.

Prayer is simply an intimate sharing between friends.
It's about frequently taking time to be alone
with the one who we know loves us.

A Woman's Heart

In an age in which women's experience was considered suspect, Teresa strongly believed that this kind of generalisation is unwarranted and that a woman's

experience should not be dismissed offhand. She herself suffered much from such harmful judgments and spiritual scaremongering. She lived and moved in the world of the spirit and encouraged others to be open to this precious gift of contemplative prayer. Contemplation is by its very nature subversive: it cannot be controlled by rules and regulations and will always threaten established structures and expected standards.

Teresa can probably not be called a feminist as we understand the term today, and might be ill at ease with those who claim her as their champion, but she was every inch a woman secure in her own calling. She showed by her spirit of courage and determination the hidden riches and untapped potential within every woman's heart. She discovered a freedom for herself and for her sisters that was grounded in the discovery of an authentic self. The more the embrace of God enfolded her, the more glorious was her discovery of who she was as a woman loved by

God. She was not afraid to risk the adventure that drew her evermore deeply into her own centre and into the presence of her Beloved. Love cherished the feminine in her and lifted her up to the embrace of that love.

> *Prayer is an exercise of love.*
> *Do whatever most nourishes love.*

A New Way

Teresa was not afraid to forge her own way or take the road less travelled. In asserting the right of a handful of women to follow their own way of life, she was asserting the dignity and equality of all men and women to take their rightful place in the world and live their lives in the joy and freedom of their own particular calling. She calls out to every woman, in whatever way of life she has chosen, to realise her own truth, to follow the deepest longing of her heart, and let the beauty and wisdom of a woman's heart enrich and transform a world in waiting.

In her journey towards wholeness Teresa found God and herself. If her life has any meaning, it is surely an invitation and a reminder that we, too, can do the same.

A Time for Penance

One day, Teresa was being hosted by a
wealthy patroness, who offered her a
portion of roast partridge which Teresa
gladly accepted. One of the other nuns was
shocked. Seeing the scandalised look on her
face, Teresa said to her: 'There's a time for
penance and a time for partridge!' Then she
returned to the tasty dish.

Let Nothing Trouble You

Let nothing trouble you
Let nothing disturb you
All things pass away
God never changes
Patience obtains all things
The one who has God lacks nothing
God alone suffices

(Teresa's 'Bookmark')

Anxiety is so pervasive that we accept it as we accept traffic jams, air pollution or the weather forecast. And it seldom comes alone – a whole family of unwanted guests tag along, for tension, fear and worry are never far behind. Willpower cannot master it, and if it is suppressed it will erupt unannounced in all sorts of negative and disordered emotions. Is there a cause and is there a solution? Teresa seems to think so. But the answer is so simple and yet so radical that we either dismiss it or fail to accept it.

Time and Eternity

Teresa's 'Bookmark', as it is called, is her meditation on the daily struggle of life, facing the great imponderables – time and eternity – and searching for a meaning that will make sense of it all. This reflection was found after her death, inserted into the pages of her breviary. It seems to have been written spontaneously, a flash of insight, a burst of inspiration. We have no idea where or when it was written, nor does it matter. It stands alone, complete in itself, and captures an eternal truth outside time and place.

The most striking thing about the 'Bookmark' is that she wrote it for herself, not at the request of others or for any of her countless friends and correspondents. They are her own words, not words she read in a book or words spoken to her by our Lord, as often happened. They are unique in their brevity and simplicity and reveal something of Teresa in a way few of her other writings do. How often she must have pondered the words, repeating them like a mantra, finding solace and courage in their simplicity and in their depth.

Truth suffers, but never dies.

A Universal Truth

Written in a moment of anxiety or of questioning, Teresa needed to remind herself of what was important and permanent against the background of the confusion and turmoil that so often surrounded her. This is not Teresa, the great teacher of prayer or the assured spiritual guide.

This is a woman, looking back over the years, reflecting on the meaning of life, life in the raw without frills or extras, wrestling with the questions as she intuits a response.

But the real power of her words is seen from how easily we recognise them for what they are: words that resonate within our own lives and speak to our own restless hearts. They hold a universal truth and are a sober reminder of an unchanging reality: the nature of impermanence. All things pass away, time itself is passing, and life flows on in its inexorable movement towards its own fulfilment. What matters is not time but presence and the seasons of the heart, an awareness of things coming and going, things past and things yet to come, gathered into the present moment and the eternal 'now'.

This is no more than what every great teacher and wisdom figure in every age, tradition and culture has placed before us. But Teresa is not interested in philosophy or in theories; it is a question of inviting us not to be afraid to look deeply into our own hearts. For her, the one ever-present reality is God – unchanging, ever new – and the underlying love and providence that hold all things in his care. He finds his home not only in our hearts, but in the day-to-day reality of our messy, troubled, anxiety-filled lives.

> *Some people think that they will lose all devotion*
> *if they relax a little.*

A Meditation on Anxiety

But perhaps the greater task and challenge is to 'let nothing trouble you!' Is Teresa for real? Has she any idea of the burden of troubles that settle, each day, on our shoulders? Ours is an age of anxiety, and it comes in all shapes and sizes.

Whatever we say about Teresa, we cannot accuse her of being out of touch with reality: mystic she certainly was, but an earthy one. Practical and pragmatic, she never left the world of human experience. She had enough troubles herself to fill the whole of Spain! But she saw clearly the root cause of much of our anxiety. It is not some minor irritant occasioned by accident or circumstance. It is anxiety about God: an anxiety that doubts his love, that questions his care and competence. It gives rise to a quiet disbelief in our own value and the ultimate purpose of our lives.

Faith, for Teresa, is not anxiety under sedation! It is a dynamic response to even the most fundamental questions and challenges. It is a message straight from the Gospel itself: 'Do not let your hearts be troubled. Trust in God still, and trust in me' (Jn 14:1). This is a pearl of great price, for which all other counterfeit pearls must be cast aside. A saying attributed to her captures beautifully the vitality and assurance of her vision: 'He knows all things, he can do all things and he loves me!'

*May the Lord make you as holy as I ask him to do
and watch over you for my sake;
for, as bad as you are, I wish I had more like you!*

Words of Wisdom

When she wrote the 'Bookmark', Teresa must have been troubled and afraid, fragile, vulnerable, perhaps at her wits' end. No great revelation to reassure her, only the pithy phrases she needed to hold onto, a raw and naked faith and boundless trust. Perhaps it is here as nowhere else that we can identify so closely with her; she stands with us on our own ground. Her words of wisdom and truth echo down the years, borne on the wings of the Spirit – words we can make our own, carrying them like a refrain in the anxious searching of our own hearts:

Let nothing trouble you
Let nothing disturb you
All things pass away
God never changes
Patience obtains all things
The one who has God lacks nothing
God alone suffices

A Life Overwhelmed by a Presence

What can Teresa of Avila teach us five hundred years after her birth? Her greatest legacy is the genius of her life – a life lived fully and totally for God. She opens up for us a world of divine intimacy, a world we often choose to ignore or fail to explore. A cloistered nun, she entered the world of countless men and women, shedding light and wisdom, with both humour and common sense. She shared her humanity with the world, and the world opened its heart to the wisdom and experience of a gifted life.

She herself started at the bottom, spending a long time on the plain and doing her best to resist the invitation of grace! She charted her turbulent journey with clarity and ruthless honesty in a way that today still touches every pilgrim heart and seeker of truth. Teresa's magnetic personality can sometimes overshadow her tender compassion and sensitive understanding of the realities of life in the raw. She abhorred gloomy, self-important orthodoxy, asking unashamedly to be delivered from sour-faced saints! Hers is a sanctity that attracts rather than deters; she makes the difficult seem possible and has nothing but words of encouragement for strugglers and battlers like herself.

> *It is foolish for you to be worried about perfection*
> *when you should be looking after yourself.*
> *For your health is important.*

A Woman for Our Times

'Mystic' and 'contemplative' are the terms usually associated with Teresa but she was also an immensely practical and capable woman, which makes her very much a saint for our times. She lived parallel lives: she was an astute businesswoman and negotiator, yet she explored uncharted regions of the spirit and was able to record with grace and precision the wondrous beauty of the inner castle of her own soul.

Teresa knew that our inner and outer lives need each other. Seldom have Martha and Mary walked together so effortlessly in the service of God and of others. Teresa put God first and encourages us to do the same: 'God alone suffices.' Life is worth living, it has meaning. The invitation is to grow, and to live life to the full. In a world where time and money control our every waking thought, she asks us to take God seriously and to free up our hearts for the deeper things that really nourish us: prayer, silence and simplicity. Prayer is not dependent on rules or methods. Nothing kills prayer as quickly as a dull sense of duty. It is a conversation with someone who we know loves us, a sharing between friends. 'Do whatever fosters love' could be Teresa's motto. Prayer is a way of life: we pray the way we live, and we live the way we pray.

> *Lord, how you afflict your lovers!*
> *But it is small in comparison*
> *with what you give them afterwards.*

A Lover's Quest

Where did Teresa find the inspiration and enthusiasm to pour out her life and share her prolific talents with the world about her? For her, the answer is simple. Like every saint, she found her way into the heart of Christ and fell in love with him. She was captivated by his love and overwhelmed by his presence. How utterly simple are her words: 'I have been deeply devoted to Christ all my life.' He was her companion at every turn of the road, her guide and fellow traveller, a 'forever friend'. Not only was she a lover of Christ but, through him, she learned to love all things human, which is possibly a much rarer vocation and gift of grace.

It seems quite natural to explain the saints in the light of Christ, but it is also important to explain Christ in the light of the saints. Christ lived before Christianity; the saints live in times, and in places familiar to us. They bring him near to us, translate him into our everyday experience and culture, and make him present in a world far removed from first-century Palestine. They look at the world each day with fresh eyes – a world, for them, charged with the radiance of his presence and his love.

There is nothing secondary about the place of Christ in Teresa's life. Love and friendship influenced her entire relationship with him. She loved to meditate on Christ present within her. She was never afraid of the questions he would ask or the tears she might shed. He was for her the 'Good Jesus', the source and fount of all she ever wanted to be, the fulfilment of all her searching: 'What more could we want than to have such a companion at our side?' As the full splendour of his presence in her life was revealed to her, she was more and more overwhelmed by the tenderness and intimacy of his love. She did not see him with the eyes of the body, but far more clearly, with those of the soul.

> *The important thing is not to think much*
> *but to love much.*

Friendship with Christ

Without Christ we cannot understand Teresa's life or her teaching. His presence permeated her whole being, not just during prayer but in the midst of her busy life, with all its difficulties and struggles. Often he revealed his presence to her in the everyday events of life, spoke a word of comfort or enlightenment and let her know, in countless little ways, of his guiding and protecting hand.

Teresa's writings stand as a powerful witness to the fact that whatever gospel road we travel, the only true way is through Christ. She is ready to defend her position against all comers, even the learned theologians of her day. There is a practical humility about Teresa that wants no way other than that taken by God himself – a sane, common-sense pragmatism that accepts the reality of the human situation: 'We are not angels. We have these bodies. It's crazy to desire to be angels while we are still on earth, especially if we are as earthbound as I was!'

*I can find nothing with which to compare
the beauty of the soul and its great capacity.*

Immortal Diamond

In her beautiful poem 'The Summer Day', Mary Oliver asks this searching question: 'Tell me, what is it you plan to do with your one, wild and precious life?' Teresa asked the same question and found the answer within her own heart. She is a witness to a forgotten world: the reality of the spiritual. Her story is ours. She shares not only a journey and a discovery but a dream: God's dream for us. We are called to greatness and to the fullness of new life.

Ours is an anxious, troubled world but also a beautiful world, filled with meaning, purpose and adventure. Putting God at the centre of that world is the beginning; placing ourselves firmly on the road is the challenge. We are called to explore the wonders hidden in our own heart – the still-point of our turning world, the immortal diamond. It is never a journey we make on our own: it is a two-way shared adventure. We are not walking away from life but discovering the things that matter most – a simple equation of putting God at the centre of all we do and all we are.

But we are also called to explore and confront the larger, wider world in which we live. Teresa lived in dark and turbulent days – an age, like our own, of doubt and confusion. Everything was against her: she was a woman of no importance, with little education and even fewer resources. But she met opposition with the most effective weapons at her disposal: her charm, her courage and her boundless trust in God. A passionate lover of Christ, she became a servant of his love; and love, in the end, is the only thing that matters.

Is it any wonder that today, five hundred years after her birth, she is still the liveliest, the most accessible, and one of the most delightful of all the saints – an earthy mystic who walked with God yet never lost the common touch, a woman of deep spirituality, fully human and fully alive.

To Teresa

They will remember you.
They will forget the bishops and the archbishops,
the theologians and the Grand Inquisitor,
but they will remember the nun in the patched habit
who was gracious and gay
and had no use for long-faced saints.
And others coming after in other countries
and in another age will marvel,
looking back across the centuries,
at how this woman, who while still on earth
had foretaste of the joys of heaven,
was no less human than themselves.

(Elizabeth Hamilton)

Text Credits

The Collected Works of St Teresa of Avila, 3 volumes,
translated by Kieran Kavanaugh OCD & Otilio
Rodriguez OCD, Washington, DC: ICS
Publications, 1987, 1980 & 1985.

The Collected Letters of St Teresa of Avila, 2 volumes,
translated by Kieran Kavanaugh OCD,
Washington, DC: ICS Publications, 2001 & 2007.

The Complete Works of Saint Teresa of Jesus, 3 volumes,
translated and edited by E. Allison Peers, London:
Sheed & Ward, 1946.

The Letters of Saint Teresa of Jesus, 2 volumes, translated
and edited by E. Allison Peers, London: Burns,
Oates & Washbourne, 1951.

Teresa of Ávila: The Book of My Life, translated by
    Mirabai Starr, Boston & London: New Seeds,
    2007.
Hamilton, Elizabeth, *The Great Teresa*, London: Chatto
    & Windus, 1960.

Note: Some of the quotations and stories from the life of
St Teresa are taken from the tradition and folklore of the
Carmelite Order.